The Science of a Glass of Water

The Science of
States of Matter

By Anna Claybourne

Science and Curriculum Consultant:
Debra Voege, M.A., *Science Curriculum Resource Teacher*

Gareth Stevens
Publishing

Please visit our web site at **www.garethstevens.com**.
For a free color catalog describing Gareth Stevens Publishing's list of high-quality books,
call 1-800-542-2595 (USA) or 1-800-387-3178 (Canada). Gareth Stevens Publishing's fax: 1-877-542-2596

Library of Congress Cataloging-in-Publication Data
Claybourne, Anna.
    The science of a glass of water : the science of states of matter / by Anna Claybourne.
        p. cm. — (The science of ?)
    Includes bibliographical references and index.
    ISBN-10: 1-4339-0041-6   ISBN-13: 978-1-4339-0041-9 (lib. bdg. : alk. paper)
     1. Matter—Properties—Experiments—Juvenile literature. 2. Science—Experiments—
Juvenile literature. 3. Water—Experiments—Juvenile literature. I. Title.
    QC173.36.C59   2008
    530.4078—dc22   2008034028

This North American edition first published in 2009 by
Gareth Stevens Publishing
A Weekly Reader® Company
1 Reader's Digest Road
Pleasantville, NY 10570-7000 USA

This U.S. edition copyright © 2009 by Gareth Stevens, Inc.
Original edition copyright © 2008 by Franklin Watts. First published in Great Britain
in 2008 by Franklin Watts, 338 Euston Road, London NW1 3BH, United Kingdom.

For Discovery Books Limited:
Editor: Rebecca Hunter   Designer: Keith Williams
Illustrator: Stefan Chabluk   Photo researcher: Rachel Tisdale

Gareth Stevens Executive Managing Editor: Lisa M. Herrington
Gareth Stevens Senior Editor: Barbara Bakowski
Gareth Stevens Creative Director: Lisa Donovan
Gareth Stevens Cover Designer: Keith Plechaty
Gareth Stevens Electronic Production Manager: Paul Bodley
Gareth Stevens Publisher: Keith Garton
Special thanks to Laura Anastasia, Michelle Castro, and Jennifer Ryder-Talbot

Photo credits: Shutterstock, cover; Discovery Picture Library, p. 4 top; istockphoto.com/Gene Chutka, p. 4 bottom; istockphoto.com/Henk Badenhorst, p. 5; istockphoto.com/Tatiana Grozetskaya, p. 6; stockphoto.com/Graham Clarke, p. 7; CFW Images/Michael Huggan, p. 9 top; NASA, p. 9 bottom; Getty Images/Paul Nicklen/National Geographic, p. 10; istockphoto.com/Anika Salsera, p. 12; istockphoto.com/Celso Pupo Rodrigues, p. 13; istockphoto.com/Anna Bryukhanova, p. 14; istockphoto.com/ddbell, p. 15; The University of Georgia, p.16; istockphoto.com/Paul Prescott, p. 18 top right; istockphoto.com/Paul Vasarhelyi, p. 18 bottom right; istockphoto.com/MaleWitch, p. 18 top left; istockphoto.com/Purdue9394, p. 18 bottom left; Corbis/Bettmann, p. 19 left; istockphoto.com/Sebastian Santa, p. 19 right; istockphoto.com/Celso Diniz, p. 20; istockphoto.com/Bill Grove, p.22; CFW Images/Edward Parker, p. 23; istockphoto.com/Gerald Bernard, p. 24; istockphoto.com/draschwartz, p. 27 top; istockphoto.com/Sean Randall, p. 27 bottom; istockphoto.com/Chanyut Sribuarawd, p. 28; istockphoto.com/Klaas Lingbeek-van Kranen, p. 29. Every effort has been made to trace copyright holders. We apologize for any inadvertent omissions and would be pleased to insert appropriate acknowledgments in a subsequent edition.

Printed in the United States of America
1 2 3 4 5 6 7 8 9 10 09 08

Contents

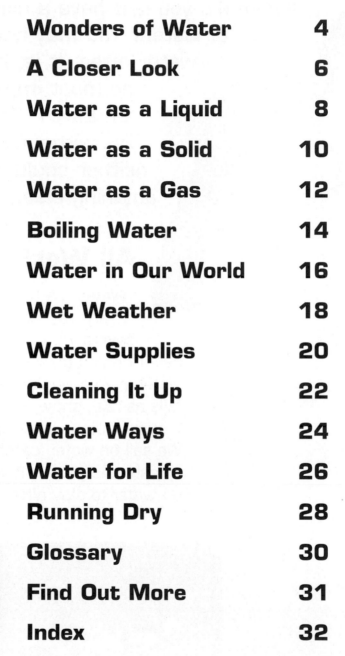

Words that appear in **boldface** type are in the glossary on page 30.

Wonders of Water

When did you last have a clear, cool glass of water? You may not think about water often. It is, however, one of the most important things on Earth. You couldn't live without water—and neither could anyone or anything else.

All Wet!

Water is a huge part of our lives. Every day, each person takes in several quarts of it. (Even if you never drink a glass of water, you take in water in your drinks and your food.) Water falls as rain, snow, sleet, and hail. It surrounds us in the seas and oceans. We sail on water, catch fish in it, and swim, splash, and play in it. All living things rely on water to stay alive.

▲ *Everyone should drink several glasses of water each day.*

▶ *Water is necessary in our lives. It can be fun, too!*

▲ *A lot of water that is moving at once, like this big wave, can be powerful and scary.*

Water World

When you pour a glass of water, do you know where it comes from? Do you know what is in it? When you turn on the faucet, water comes out—but how did it get there?

Read on to find the answers. Learn what water is, why we need it, and how we use it. Dive in to explore the science and technology that goes into delivering water to your home, to your tap, and, finally, to the glass in your hand.

Dangerous Water

We need water, but too much of it can cause serious problems. For example, floods ruin homes and crops. Strong waves that crash onto shores sweep away villages and towns. Rising seas swallow up land. People die by drowning. Dirty water sometimes carries deadly diseases.

A Closer Look

A glass of water looks clear, but what is it made of? Like everything else, water is made of tiny bits called **atoms** and **molecules**. The number of molecules in a glass of water is huge!

Atoms and Molecules

All the materials around us, including water, wood, plastic, and stone, are made of atoms. Atoms are tiny particles. They are so small that you can't see them. There are about 100 different types of atoms. Water contains two types of atoms—**oxygen** atoms and **hydrogen** atoms.

▼ *As this stream flows, trillions of water molecules rush over the rocks every second.*

Atoms often join to make bigger particles called molecules. Water is made up of water molecules. Each water molecule is made up of two hydrogen (H) atoms and one oxygen (O) atom. Scientists write this as H_2O.

What Else Is in Water?

Pure water contains only water molecules. It has no taste, smell, or color. Most water in the world, however, is not pure. The water in rivers and lakes contains dirt, insects, and leaves. It also contains tiny living things such as **bacteria** and **algae**. Water in the oceans is not pure, either. It contains salt.

The water that comes out of your faucet at home has been cleaned. But it still contains substances such as chemicals that are added to kill germs.

Water naturally contains some **minerals**, such as calcium. Many communities add **fluoride** to water to prevent tooth decay.

◄ Oxygen (O) atoms

Hydrogen (H) atoms ►

◄ Water molecule (H_2O)

There are trillions of water molecules in one glass of water. ►

Did You Know?

There are more molecules in one glass of water than there are glasses of water in all the world's seas and oceans!

Water as a Liquid

Water is a liquid. It can be poured into a glass. It can splash, spill, and drip. Water can take other forms, too. When water gets very cold, it freezes into a solid—ice. When water is heated, it can become a gas and escape into the air.

Three Forms of Water

Water can take three forms—solid, liquid, and gas. Its temperature—how hot or cold it is—determines the form water takes.

When water reaches its freezing point, it becomes solid ice. The freezing point of water is 32° Fahrenheit (0° Celsius).

When water is heated until it boils, some molecules escape from the surface. They float into the air as a gas called **water vapor**. Water boils at 212° F (100° C).

▲ *Although the molecules in liquid water can move about easily, they remain fairly close together.*

What Is a Liquid?

In a liquid, molecules can move freely. They slip and slide against one another as they move about. Because of the movement of its molecules, liquid water flows, forms puddles, and takes the shape of any container.

Liquid Planet

On most of Earth, the temperature is usually between the freezing point and the boiling point of water. Living things survive because they can get plenty of liquid water, although only a small portion of Earth's water is fresh.

▶ *Like all living things, zebras need water to survive.*

The Power to Dissolve

Liquid water can dissolve many materials. It breaks them down into molecules that combine with the water. For example, soft drinks are mostly water with other substances dissolved in it. These are called **solutions**.

Sometimes, tiny bits of a substance are mixed into the water without dissolving. This forms a **suspension**. For example, muddy or sandy water has soil particles suspended in it.

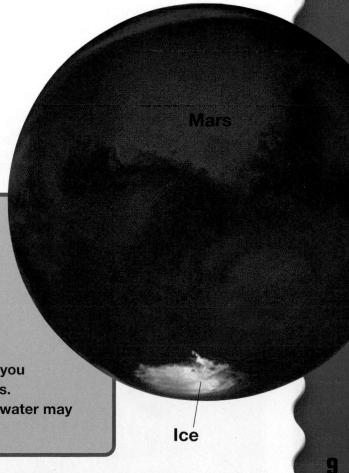

Mars

Ice

Water on Other Planets

The other planets in our **solar system** have water, but they are too hot or too cold for water to exist as a liquid. For example, water exists in the form of a gas on Venus, which is very hot. Mars is much colder than Earth, so the water on Mars is frozen as ice. At the bottom of this photo, you can see some of the ice on the planet Mars. Scientists have found evidence that liquid water may have once existed on Mars.

Water as a Solid

On a hot summer day, you might add a few ice cubes to your glass of water to cool it. Ice is water that has frozen, or turned into a solid.

All About Ice

When water is cooled to its freezing point, the molecules stop flowing freely. They begin to fix themselves into a regular pattern. As this happens, the molecules spread out a bit. The water expands, or takes up more space, as it freezes. Ice is less **dense**, so it is lighter than liquid water. That is why icebergs float in the sea and why ice-covered lakes and ponds shelter fish in the liquid water below.

Most substances shrink as they get colder. When they change from a liquid into a solid, they get denser and heavier. Solid butter, for example, does not float on melted butter. It sinks.

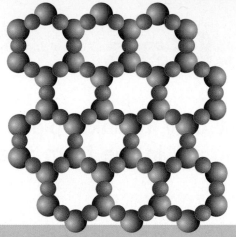

▲ *The molecules in frozen water are locked together in a regular pattern.*

Slip Sliding Away

Why is ice slippery? Scientists believe that ice has a very thin layer of water on its surface. A few molecules stay loose and flowing, like liquid water. This thin layer makes it hard for shoes and car tires to grip the ice.

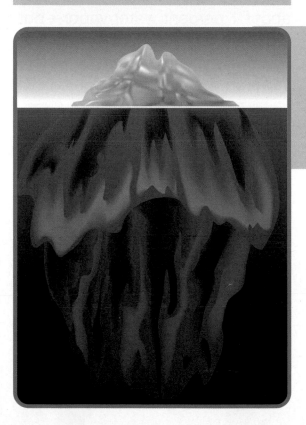

◄ *Icebergs are dangerous to ships. When ice floats in water, about nine-tenths of the ice is beneath the surface. Only one-tenth is visible.*

How Water Breaks Rock

Did you know that water can split a rock into pieces? Liquid water seeps into tiny cracks in rocks. If the temperature drops below 32° F (0° C), the water freezes and expands. It slowly pushes the cracks apart, making them wider. Eventually, a piece of the rock breaks off. This process is called **ice weathering**. Over many years, ice weathering can damage stone walls and statues. It can even wear away mountains.

◄ *An iceberg is a chunk of ice that has broken away from a **glacier** and floated into the sea. The ice floats because it is lighter than liquid water.*

Water as a Gas

Water is all around you. It is not only in sinks, pipes, rivers, and lakes. It is also in the air, in the form of an invisible gas called water vapor.

Evaporation

When you heat a pot of water to its boiling point, 212° F (100° C), the water molecules move quickly. Some **evaporate**, or turn into water vapor.

Water can also evaporate at other temperatures. Some molecules have enough **energy** to escape from the surface of liquid water and become water vapor in the air.

The warmer the water is, the more easily it evaporates. Air is normally about 1 percent water vapor—but it can hold more or less water. **Humidity** is the amount of water vapor in the air.

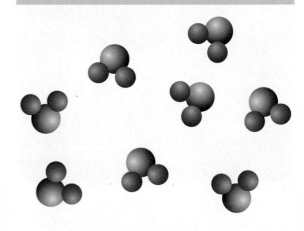

▼ *In water vapor, as in other gases, the molecules are spread far apart and move about quickly.*

◀ *The Sun provides heat to evaporate the water in laundry that is hung outdoors to dry.*

Condensation

When water vapor gets cold, it **condenses**, or turns back into a liquid. You can see condensation happening if you take a cold can out of the refrigerator on a warm day. Water vapor in the air condenses on the cold can, covering it with liquid water droplets.

Sweating It Out

Water molecules need energy to break free from liquid water and become water vapor. The molecules get energy in the form of heat from their surroundings.

Our bodies use this process to help us cool down when we get too hot. Our skin releases liquid sweat. It sits on the surface of the warm skin and starts to evaporate. As the sweat evaporates, it takes heat from the skin. The body cools down.

Before Your Eyes

Have you ever seen your breath in the air on a cold day? What you see is the water in your warm breath. Normally, your breath is invisible. In cold air, the water vapor starts to condense. It forms tiny water droplets that you can see. Your breath becomes a mini-cloud in front of your face!

▼ *Water vapor in the warm air condenses and collects on cold cans.*

Boiling Water

In prehistoric times, people found that food is easier to eat—and it tastes better—when it is cooked. We often use boiling water to cook food. Boiling water has a lot of other uses, too.

In Hot Water

If you look around your home or school, you will probably see plenty of uses for boiling water. You may boil water to make hot drinks and to cook food. You may also have a boiler that heats water to warm your home and provide hot water for baths and showers.

Why Heat Cooks

A raw potato is hard, and it is not delicious. What happens if you cook that potato in boiling water for 20 minutes? It becomes soft and tasty! When food is heated, the chemicals in it change. The molecules in food break apart and may form new chemicals. This process changes the form and flavor of the food. So cooked food tastes different from raw food. Reheated food can taste different from food that has been heated only once.

▲ *People often boil water to cook food, such as eggs.*

Hot Water in the Wild

Most water in nature is cold. But in areas near volcanoes, water may be heated by hot melted rock inside Earth. In **geysers**, boiling water and steam burst through cracks in Earth's surface. At the bottom of the ocean, **superheated** water escapes from the seabed at **hydrothermal vents**.

Useful Energy

Did you know that most of the electricity in the United States is made by boiling water? A fuel such as coal is burned to heat water to produce steam. The steam pushes at the blades of an engine called a **turbine**, making it whirl around. The turbine is connected to a **generator**. A generator is a device that changes the spinning motion of the turbine into electricity. The electric power is carried through wires to homes and businesses.

▲ *A geyser is a natural boiling water fountain! Hot rock heats water in an underground pool. When the water boils, it shoots out of the ground as a giant jet.*

▼ *In a power station, fuel is burned to boil water to make steam. The steam turns a turbine, and a generator changes the turning motion into electricity.*

Power Station

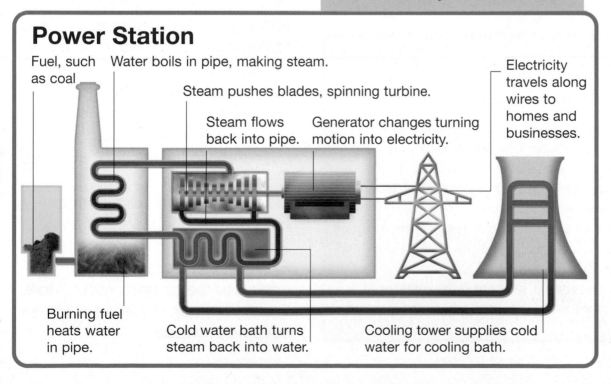

Fuel, such as coal

Water boils in pipe, making steam.

Steam pushes blades, spinning turbine.

Steam flows back into pipe.

Generator changes turning motion into electricity.

Electricity travels along wires to homes and businesses.

Burning fuel heats water in pipe.

Cold water bath turns steam back into water.

Cooling tower supplies cold water for cooling bath.

Water in Our World

Where did the water in your glass come from? It might have come from a tap in your home. The water in the tap came from rain. Where did it come from before that? The surprising answer is ... outer space!

▲ Of all the water on Earth, 97 percent of it is in the seas and oceans.

In the Beginning

Scientists think Earth formed about 4.5 billion years ago. Dust, rocks, and hot gases in space clumped together. One of the gases was water vapor. As Earth cooled, the vapor turned into liquid water. It fell as rain and collected on the planet's surface.

More water came from comets— balls of rock and ice that flew through space. When comets hit Earth, the ice in them melted, adding to the planet's water. More than two-thirds of Earth's surface is covered in water.

Water, Water Everywhere

Earth is called the Blue Planet for a reason. Water covers about 70 percent of Earth's surface.

- About 97 percent of that water is in the seas and oceans.
- About 2 percent is frozen as ice around the North Pole and the South Pole and on high mountains.
- Less than 1 percent is freshwater in rivers and lakes and under the ground.

Seas and Oceans

Earth is covered in a rocky layer called the **crust**. All the water on the planet flows downward. It is pulled by the force of **gravity** toward the center of Earth. Over time, water has filled the places where Earth's crust is lowest, forming the seas and oceans.

▼ *The diagram below shows a simplified version of the water cycle.*

The Water Cycle

Water doesn't just stay in one place. It constantly moves from the oceans to the air, to the land, and back to the oceans again. This unending pattern is called the **water cycle**.

Ancient Water

The water cycle has been happening for billions of years. The amount of water on Earth doesn't change. The water in your glass might have satisfied the thirst of a dinosaur!

The Water Cycle

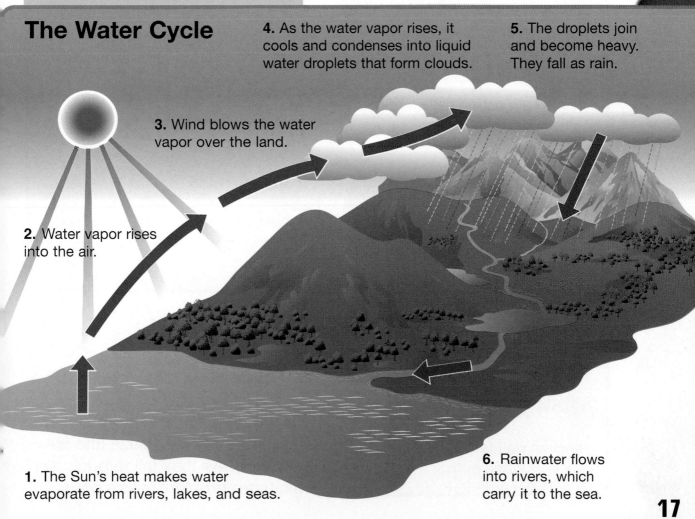

4. As the water vapor rises, it cools and condenses into liquid water droplets that form clouds.

5. The droplets join and become heavy. They fall as rain.

3. Wind blows the water vapor over the land.

2. Water vapor rises into the air.

1. The Sun's heat makes water evaporate from rivers, lakes, and seas.

6. Rainwater flows into rivers, which carry it to the sea.

Wet Weather

Water usually falls from the sky as rain. It can also fall as snow, sleet, or hail. Dew, frost, and fog are all forms of water, too. Water plays a big role in most kinds of weather. Any form of water that falls from the sky is called **precipitation**.

Cloud Shapes

Clouds are made of water vapor that has condensed into tiny water droplets. The droplets are not heavy enough to fall to the ground. The air holds them up. Clouds look like fluffy puffs of steam or smoke.

Clouds form different shapes, depending on the weather and their height in the sky.

Stratus clouds are wide, flat layers that block out sunlight.

Low, dark nimbus clouds usually signal rain.

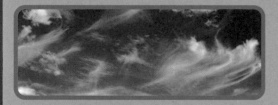

Thin, wispy cirrus clouds form high in the sky.

Cumulus clouds float lower and look like cotton puffs.

Snow Days

If the air temperature is 32° F (0° C) or lower, water can freeze before it reaches the ground. Snowflakes form when tiny droplets of water freeze into ice **crystals**. As they fall through the air, more droplets freeze onto

▲ *All snowflakes have a six-sided shape, but no two flakes are exactly the same.*

▲ *In an ice storm, a thick layer of ice can build up on trees, making branches snap.*

them, building up a six-sided pattern. The crystals may join to form fluffy snowflakes.

Hailstones are hard, heavy balls of ice. They form in thunderclouds when water freezes around specks of dust. As layers of ice build up, the hailstones grow bigger and heavier. Finally, they fall to the ground.

Dew, Frost, and Fog

On some mornings, the ground is wet although no rain has fallen. The moisture is dew. It forms when water vapor in the air condenses on the cold ground. At cold temperatures, dew can freeze, making frost. If water vapor condenses into little droplets in the air, it creates fog.

Ice Storms

An ice storm happens when liquid rain falls onto freezing-cold ground. As the rain hits the ground, it freezes. Everything is covered with a layer of heavy, slippery ice. The ice can make people slip and cars skid. It can also weigh down trees and power lines until they break.

Over the Rainbow

Did you know that a rainbow is simply water? When you see a rainbow, you are looking at sunlight shining through raindrops. The curved shape of a raindrop splits the white sunlight into a band of colors.

Water Supplies

Have you thought about what happens to water before it flows out of your tap? It doesn't get there by magic! It must be collected, stored, cleaned, and then piped to your home.

Collecting Water

Water is collected and stored in big, human-made lakes called **reservoirs**. There is always water ready to use, even when the weather is dry.

Some reservoirs are made by building a dam across a river. A dam is a strong wall that holds back water, creating a big lake.

Dams: Good or Bad?

In addition to creating reservoirs, dams can help make electricity. At a **hydroelectric power** plant, water is let through a dam at high speed. The water turns a turbine, and a generator changes the turning power into electricity. Hydroelectric power is good for the environment because it creates little **pollution**.

▼ *The Hoover Dam is on the Colorado River between Nevada and Arizona. The dam runs a hydroelectric power plant that supplies electricity to people in Nevada, Arizona, and California.*

Water From the Sea

In some dry countries, there is so little rain that people cannot get enough water from rivers or underground supplies. Instead, they take water from the sea. The water must be **desalinated** (treated to remove the salt) before people can drink it.

Building a dam can also harm the environment. To make a dam, workers must flood a large area of land with water. That process can harm animal and plant **habitats**. Some dams cause problems for towns and villages.

Water From Down Under

When rain falls, water soaks deep into underground rocks. This water is called **groundwater**. People can collect it by digging wells and pumping the water up to the surface.

Down the Pipe

Most reservoirs are higher than the towns and cities that rely on them for water. Water reaches those cities by flowing downhill. Gravity helps provide pressure to push the water through the pipes.

▼ *This diagram shows how a hydroelectric dam works. Water flows through the dam and turns a turbine to make electricity.*

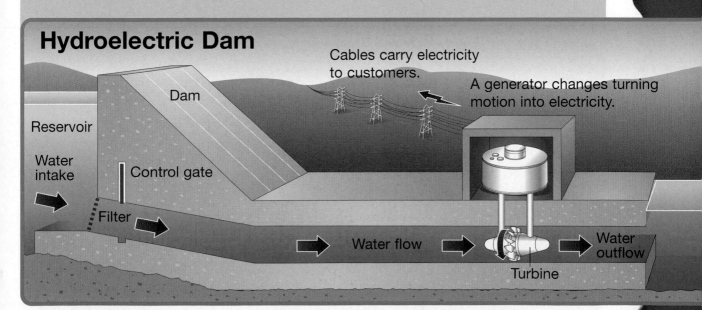

Hydroelectric Dam

Cables carry electricity to customers.

A generator changes turning motion into electricity.

Dam

Reservoir

Water intake

Control gate

Filter

Water flow

Turbine

Water outflow

Cleaning It Up

Before it arrives at your tap, water from a reservoir must be cleaned at a **water treatment plant**. There, the water goes through several stages to make it safe for drinking.

Screening and Settling

First, the dirty water must be screened. It is passed through a big sieve, or strainer, that catches and removes objects such as twigs, insects, leaves, and litter.

Next, special chemicals are added to the water. Dirt sticks to the chemicals and clumps together. The clumps slowly sink to the bottom.

Filtering

The water is still not completely clean, so it is filtered. The water sinks slowly through layers of sand and carbon. Carbon is a black substance found in coal, for example. The carbon soaks up germs and smells, and the sand filters out any remaining bits of dirt.

The clean water passes on to the next stage.

▼ *A water treatment plant, as seen from an airplane*

Killing Germs

Before the water is ready for drinking, a chemical called chlorine must be added. This is the same chemical used in swimming pools. (There is much less chlorine in drinking water than in pool water.) Chlorine kills germs in the water.

Sometimes, other chemicals are also added. For example, some drinking water contains fluoride, a substance that helps prevent tooth decay.

Into the Mains

From the water treatment plant, treated water flows into **mains**. These big underground pipes carry water through cities and towns to homes and buildings.

Water Treatment Plant

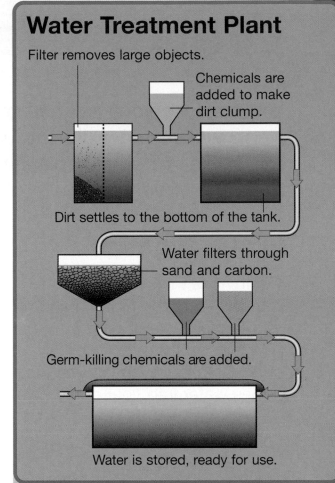

Filter removes large objects.

Chemicals are added to make dirt clump.

Dirt settles to the bottom of the tank.

Water filters through sand and carbon.

Germ-killing chemicals are added.

Water is stored, ready for use.

▲ *Water goes through several stages at a treatment plant.*

Untreated Water

Long ago, people collected water straight from a river or a well. In some parts of the world, people still get water in that way. Their countries or communities are too poor to build treatment plants and pipes. Untreated water may contain dirt or germs that cause disease.

Water Ways

You turn on your kitchen faucet and fill a glass with clean water. How did the water get from the main in the street to your tap—and how does water flow to the rest of your home?

In the Pipeline

Plumbing is the system of pipes that carries water into and around your home. A water pipe branches off from the public water main in the street. The pipe carries water into your home. It is connected to other pipes that lead to the faucets in your kitchen and bathroom. Pipes also carry water to your shower, heating system, washing machine, and toilet.

Go With the Flow

The water in the main is under **pressure**, so it constantly pushes up into your home's plumbing. Why doesn't water flow out of the taps nonstop? When a tap is turned off, it is sealed shut by a flat, thin ring-shaped part inside it. When you turn on the tap, this part moves, creating an opening through which the water flows.

◄ *You probably turn on the tap whenever you want a glass of water. Now you know how much work it takes to get the water to your kitchen!*

Flushed Away

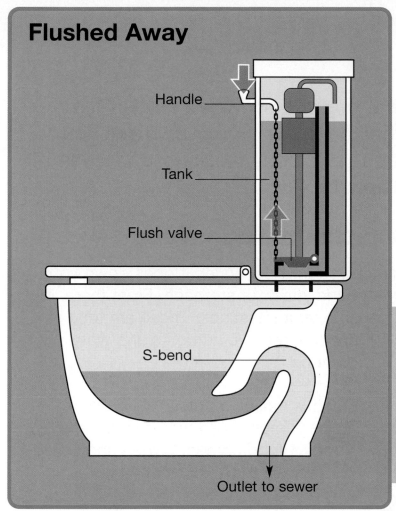

Handle

Tank

Flush valve

S-bend

Outlet to sewer

Did You Know?

Long ago, most people didn't have plumbing or sewers. They simply threw their dirty water out a window!

◀ *This diagram shows the parts of a toilet. When you press the handle, the flush valve lifts to let water empty into the bowl.*

Bowled Over

A toilet has a bowl of water linked to a curved pipe called an S-bend. The S-bend traps some water in the bowl so that it does not drain away. A toilet also has a tank that fills up with water.

When you flush the toilet, the tank empties all its water into the bowl. It sweeps away the waste through the S-bend and fills the bowl with clean water again.

Down the Drain

When you flush the toilet or pull the plug out of your bathtub drain, the dirty water is carried away through a waste pipe. The pipes that carry off wastewater are called **sewers**.

Wastewater is piped to treatment plants, where it is filtered and cleaned. The water can then be emptied into seas and rivers. Clean water can also be piped back into the water supply to be used again.

Water for Life

Now you know where a glass of water comes from—but do you know what happens to water after you drink it? Water keeps your body working and does all kinds of useful "inside jobs."

Water in Your Body

When you swallow water, it goes down your throat and into your stomach. From there, it goes into your intestines. These are tube-like organs that remove nutrients and water from food.

Blood is mostly made of water. Your heart pumps blood around your entire body. Blood carries oxygen and useful chemicals to all your body parts.

Your **cells** need water, too. They must be bathed in water to work properly. The tiny parts inside cells can do their jobs properly only when they float around in a watery solution.

70% water

◄ *Did you know that you are mostly made up of water? The human body is about 70 percent water. The water in your body does not slosh around like liquid in a pail, though! It is stored in your cells, blood, and other body fluids.*

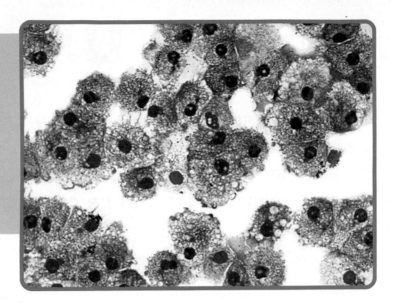

▶ *Human white blood cells can be seen under a microscope. Each cell is filled with a jelly-like material that is mostly water. Water surrounds the cells, too.*

Losing Water

You lose water from your body all the time. It comes out as sweat, saliva, tears, and water vapor in your breath. There is water in the urine that carries waste materials out of your body. You need to drink plenty of water each day to replace the water that you lose.

Animals and Plants

Humans are not the only living things that need water. Animals and plants depend on water to stay alive. Animals drink water. Plants have roots to get water from the soil.

Desert Survival

Some desert animals, such as camels, can go without drinking water for weeks! Camels store spare water in their bodies. They also save water by sweating very little.

Running Dry

All living things on Earth need water to survive. In many parts of the world, however, supplies of freshwater are running out. People are using up water more quickly than it can be replaced.

Wasting Water

There is a vast amount of water on Earth—far more than we could ever use. Most of it is salty seawater. Some water is locked up in ice. Only about 1 percent is fresh liquid water.

We have seen that the total amount of water in the world doesn't change. It constantly moves through the water cycle. Why are some scientists warning that the world is now in danger of running out of water?

More people are using more and more freshwater. Farming and industry use huge amounts of water. About 69 percent of the world's freshwater is used in farming. About 23 percent is used in industry. That leaves only 8 percent to supply all the people in all the towns and cities in the world. In some countries, freshwater is already scarce. Future climate change may affect the water supply in ways scientists cannot yet predict.

What Can We Do?

Many experts think that as water shortages get worse, people will have to use seawater. People in many countries already use desalination. The practice will probably become more common in the future.

Desalination, however, poses some problems. It is expensive, uses a lot of energy, and makes the sea saltier (because the removed salt is left behind). Wildlife in the oceans may be unable to live in saltier water.

Countries are working together to come up with solutions to the world's water shortage. We cannot increase Earth's supply of water. It is important that people use freshwater thoughtfully.

Did You Know?

More than 1 billion people—nearly one-seventh of the world's population—do not have access to a clean water supply.

You Can Save Water

You can help to save water supplies by using water carefully.
- Don't leave the water running while you brush your teeth or wash your face.
- Take quick showers instead of long baths.
- Collect rainwater or used household water to water your plants. Don't use a garden hose.
- Don't pave over land to make a driveway. Keep it as grass or soil. That will allow rain to soak deep into the ground, adding to the groundwater.

◀ It takes huge amounts of water to grow rice. Millions of tons of rice are produced around the world each day. That's a lot of rice—and a lot of water!

▲ Kuwait, a country in the Middle East, is famous for its unusual water towers. They store seawater that has been desalinated to make it safe for drinking.

Glossary

algae: tiny plant-like living things

atoms: the particles that make up all matter

bacteria: tiny living things that sometimes cause disease

cells: smallest units that make up living things

condenses: turns from a gas into a liquid

crust: the rocky outer layer of Earth

crystals: solids whose atoms or molecules are packed in an ordered, repeating pattern

dense: packed closely together

desalinated: having had the salt removed

energy: the ability to do work. Energy exists in several forms, such as heat, light, and electricity.

evaporate: to turn from a liquid into a gas

fluoride: a mineral compound that helps prevent tooth decay

freshwater: water that is drinkable and not salty

generator: a machine that converts turning motion into electricity

geysers: jets of boiling water from under the ground

glacier: a large body of ice that moves down a slope or valley or spreads outward on land

gravity: the force that pulls things toward the center of Earth

groundwater: water held in rocks underground

habitats: the places where plants or animals live in nature

humidity: the amount of water vapor in the air

hydroelectric power: electricity made by using flowing water to turn turbines

hydrogen: one of the basic substances on Earth; also one of the two ingredients of water

hydrothermal vents: holes in the seabed through which hot, boiling water escapes from inside Earth

ice weathering: the breakdown of rock caused by the expansion of water as it freezes into ice

mains: large underground pipes that carry public water supplies

minerals: solids found in nature that are not animals or plants; examples include calcium and iron

molecules: tiny particles of a substance, often made of several atoms joined together

oxygen: one of the basic substances on Earth; also one of the two ingredients of water

pollution: harmful chemicals, waste gases, or dirt released into the environment

precipitation: water that falls from the sky in the form of rain, sleet, hail, or snow

pressure: the force of one thing pressing against another thing

reservoirs: places where water is stored for later use

sewers: underground pipes that carry off wastewater

solar system: the Sun and the planets and other objects that circle it

solutions: mixtures formed by a substance dissolved in a liquid

superheated: heated above the boiling point without changing into a gas

suspension: pieces of a solid mixed into, but not dissolved in, a liquid

turbine: a wheel that can be turned by steam, flowing water, wind, or other forces to make electricity

water cycle: the movement of water on, in, and above Earth as it changes from liquid to vapor to ice and back again

water treatment plant: a place where harmful materials are removed from water to make it safe for drinking

water vapor: water in the form of a gas

Find Out More

Water Kids
www.watereducation.org/ doc.asp?id=1022
Information from the Water Education Foundation

Water Science for Schools
ga.water.usgs.gov/edu
The U.S. Geological Survey's water facts site

Publisher's note to educators and parents: Our editors have carefully reviewed these web sites to ensure that they are suitable for children. Many web sites change frequently, however, and we cannot guarantee that a site's future contents will continue to meet our high standards of quality and educational value. Be advised that children should be closely supervised whenever they access the Internet.

Index